Amazing Braids, Buns & Twists

A Step-by-Step Guide to 34 Beautiful Styles

Eric Mayost

Photography by **Roee Fainburg**

imagine! Publishing

An Imagine Book
Published by Charlesbridge
85 Main Street, Watertown, MA 02472
617-926-0329
www.charlesbridge.com

Created by Penn Publishing Ltd.

Editor-in-Chief: Rachel Penn
Edited by Shoshana Brickman
Photography by Roee Fainburg
Design and layout by Ariane Rybski
Assistant to Mr. Mayost: Ohad Zini
Styling by Raphael Cohen
Makeup by Sigal Asraf

Library of Congress Cataloging-in-Publication Data
Mayost, Eric.
Amazing braids, buns, and twists : a step-by-step guide to 34 beautiful
styles / Eric Mayost ; photography by Roee Fainburg.
    pages cm
ISBN 978-1-62354-066-1 (softcover)
ISBN 978-1-60734-951-8 (ebook)
ISBN 978-1-60734-952-5 (ebook pdf)
1. Braids (Hairdressing) I. Title.
TT975.M39 2015
646.7'24--dc23   2014033871

2 4 6 8 10 9 7 5 3 1

Contents

Introduction

Do you love long hair? If you've taken the time to grow your hair, then the answer is probably an emphatic "Yes!" Long hair is really popular these days, and it's no surprise. Healthy long hair, whether it's wavy, straight or curly, allows for so many incredible hairstyle possibilities. Long hair can be styled to look romantic, sophisticated, playful or glamorous. It can be curled or swirled, braided or wrapped, twisted or tied, and so much more. In short, the list of possibilities is as long as your hair – if not longer!

Stunning hairstyles for long hair don't have to be complicated, either. You can create salon-quality hairstyles in the comfort of your home, using just a few simple tools. All you need is inspiration and practice.

Amazing Braids, Buns & Twists is filled with fashionable ideas for your long hair (or hair that's enhanced with extensions). All the styles can be created easily in your home—no professional styling skills required. You just need freshly washed hair and a few basic supplies. You can create these hairstyles on your own hair, but you may find it easier to work with a friend. So invite someone over and learn how to create gorgeous hairstyles together. If you're planning to style your hair for a special occasion, try out the hairstyle in advance so that when the special occasion arrives, you can recreate it with ease.

Every hairstyle in **Amazing Braids, Buns & Twists** is accompanied by easy-to-follow instructions, step-by-step pictures and beautiful photos. Some of the styles include pretty accessories that can easily add a personal touch.

I hope you find plenty of inspiration and ideas in **Amazing Braids, Buns & Twists**. After all, if you've already got gorgeous long locks, you certainly want to make the most of them!

About the Author

Eric Mayost has been styling hair since he was nineteen years old. In addition to hairstyling, he studied art and graphic design. Eric has worked with some of the world's leading hairstylists and has participated in cover shoots for some of the world's leading fashion magazines.

Eric has managed his own hair salon for over a decade and is the author of **Spectacular Hair** (Sterling Publishing 2010), **Gorgeous Wedding Hairstyles** (Sterling Publishing 2012) and **Fabulous Teen Hairstyles** (Sterling Publishing 2013). He has carved a career for himself by creating out glamorous hairstyles that stars love, and he enjoys staying at the forefront of hairstyling fashion.

Braiding Glossary

The hairstyles in this book may look intricate, but they aren't. All you need are some basic braiding skills and you're ready to go. Here are a few words about the basic braids used in these designs.

3-strand (regular) braid

This braid is made with three even strands of hair. The strands can be numbered 1 to 3 and plaited together as follows: 1 over 2; 3 over 1. Re-number the strands and then bring 1 over 2; 3 over 1. Repeat until you reach the end of the hair.

4-strand braid

This braid is made with four even strands of hair. The strands can be numbered 1 to 4 and plaited together as follows: 1 over 2, 3 over 4, and then 4 over 1. Re-number the strands 1 through 4 and repeat the process: 1 over 2, 3 over 4, and then 4 over 1. Repeat until you reach the end of the hair.

French braid

This braid starts with three small strands of hair. The strands are plaited in the same pattern as a regular 3-strand braid, but each time a strand is brought over another strand, a bit more hair is incorporated into it. The top of a French braid is close to the scalp; when there is no more hair to incorporate from the scalp, a French braid is finished with a regular 3-strand braid.

Dutch braid

This braid is similar to the French braid, but rather than passing the strands over each other, the strands are passed under each other. This results in a braid that stands out from the head, rather than lying flat on it.

Fishtail braid

This braid, also known as a herringbone braid, is made with two large strands of hair. The strands can be numbered 1 and 2, and plaited together as follows: a small section from the far side of 1 is passed over 1 and integrated into 2; a small section from the far side of 2 is passed over 2 and integrated into 1. Repeat until you reach the end of the hair. The smaller the sections of hair that are passed over, the tighter the braid.

Tools & Accessories

You won't need many tools to create the hairstyles in this book, but do make sure you have the ones you need on hand before starting. The last thing you want to do is run out of bobby pins or hair elastics just as you are finishing your masterpiece hairstyle!

Blow dryer & diffuser

Use this to dry freshly washed hair before styling it.

Bobby pins & hair pins

You'll need these to secure styled hair in place. Bobby pins are U-shaped pins that have one flat side and one wavy side. The two sides are close together. Hair pins have two wavy sides that don't touch each other. Buy good quality pins, as they make all the difference when assembling your hairstyle. Also, try to find pins that match your hair color so that they are as invisible as possible in the final design.

Brushes & combs

Make sure the hair is tangle-free before you start any hairstyle. This can be tricky with long hair, so comb it out carefully before you start. A round brush is great for creating gentle curls; a paddle brush is just right for increasing volume. Use a tail comb (also known as a rattail or fine-tooth comb) to backcomb hair and make straight parts.

Curling iron

In some hairstyles, you'll need to curl the hair first, for added style and body. Practice is important when curling hair since you want to hold the iron long enough to curl the hair, but not so long that it burns it.

Hair accessories

You can use these to dress up any hairstyle that you like.

Hair clips

You'll want to have a few of these on hand to hold back sections of hair while you're styling.

Hair elastics

Use these to secure ponytails and braids. Choose ones that are gentle on the hair and don't rip it. If the hair elastics are visible in the final design, be sure to choose ones that match the color of the hair.

Hair extensions

Natural or synthetic hair additions can be integrated into hairstyles to add volume and length. If you use high quality hair extensions, they can be reused.

Hair sponge

These are integrated into hairstyles to add body and volume.

Holding spray

Spray this onto your hairstyle when it's finished to help it last as long as possible. In some cases, you'll also use holding spray during the styling process to hold a particular shape. Spray from a distance of about 8 inches so that the spray is evenly dispersed on the surface of the hair.

Elevated Elegance

This design covers all the bases: a little twist, a little fold, and some long and flowing locks.

1. Wash and blow dry the hair. Make a rounded part at the top of the head to separate the hair at the front hairline from the rest of the hair, and secure the hair in front of the part with a hair clip.

2. Grasp a strand of hair immediately behind the part and backcomb it to add volume.

3. Repeat this process, backcombing small strands of hair all the way down the back of the head.

4. Make a part that extends from the top of the right ear to the crown of the head. Working with small strands of hair every time, backcomb all the hair above the ear to add volume. Repeat this process on the left side of the head.

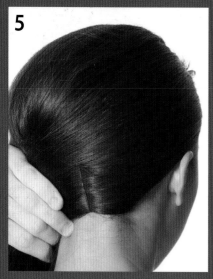

5

6

7

8

9

10

5. Gently comb all the hair on the right side of the head around the back of the head and towards the left side. Secure the hair with a vertical line of bobby pins starting at the nape of the neck.

6. Insert the bobby pins so that the open ends face upwards. Start inserting the bobby pins at the nape of the neck and work your way upwards to the crown of the head. The bobby pin at the top of the line should face downwards.

7. Now brush the hair on the left side of the head towards the back.

8. Tuck this hair over the line of bobby pins to conceal it.

9. Twist the hair downwards to make an upside-down chignon and secure with bobby pins.

10. Using a curling iron, curl the loose hair at the back of the head.

11. Release the hair at the front of the head from the hair clip. Curl the hair gently with a curling iron and then backcomb it at the roots to increase volume.

12. Gently brush this hair backwards, taking care not to reduce the volume. Pin the hair with hair clips and then mist with holding spray.

13. Grasp a small strand of the loose hair at the back of the head, on the left side.

14. Twist the hair tightly around itself to make a rope and then twist it around the hair at the back. Tuck this hair behind the loose hair and secure with bobby pins.

15. Remove the hair clips and mist with more holding spray.

11

12

13

14

15

Texture 'n' Twirls

This dramatic design includes a hair sponge to add volume. You'll twist the hair into pipes rather than ropes, which means they'll have a hollow center.

1. Wash and blow dry the hair. Make a part from the top of the left ear, over the top of the head, to the top of the right ear. Gather the hair behind the part in a high ponytail. Hold the hair in front of the part with a hair clip.

2. Wrap a hair sponge around the base of the ponytail and secure with bobby pins.

3. Release the hair at the front of the head from the hair clip. Grasp a 1-inch strand of hair at the hairline on the left and backcomb it to add volume.

4. Twist the hair around itself to make a thick pipe. Hold the ends of the twisted hair with one hand and push the hair upwards with the other hand to add volume.

5. Pin the twisted pipe of hair to the hair sponge wrapped around the ponytail.

6. Repeat this process with another strand of hair, first backcombing it, then twisting it into a thick pipe, then pushing the twisted hair back towards the head. Pin the twisted hair to the hair sponge.

7. Continue pushing back the twisted hair before pinning it to add volume and texture to the twist.

8. Repeat this process to twist and pin all the hair at the front of the head. When pinning the hair at the back, try to conceal the hair sponge as much as possible.

9. Now move to the hair in the ponytail and backcomb it to increase volume.

10. Hold the ends of the small strands of hair in the ponytail and push the hair upwards to create texture.

11. Twist the hair into a pipe, fold it towards the back of the head, and affix it with bobby pins.

12. Repeat this process with another strand of hair from the ponytail, first backcombing it to add volume, then pushing the hair upwards, twisting it and securing it at the back of the head.

13. Repeat this process with all of the hair in the ponytail.

14. First backcomb each strand, then push the hair upwards, twist it and secure.

15. Mist with holding spray. If you like, add a floral hair accessory.

11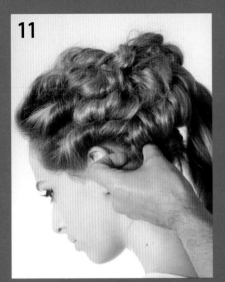

12

13

14

15

Folded Fancy

Integrate extensions to create a look that's fun, folded and textured. Perfect for an evening out!

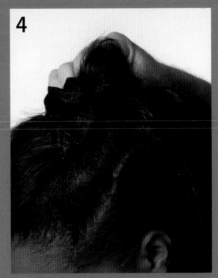

1. Wash and blow dry the hair. Divide the hair into top and bottom sections by making a part that begins at the hairline near the right eye, extends around the back of the head, and ends at the hairline above the left eye. Gather the hair above the part in a tight ponytail. Gather the hair below the part in a high ponytail just below the part.

2. Attach one hair extension immediately below the upper ponytail.

3. Attach another hair extension immediately above the lower ponytail.

4. Using a curling iron, gently curl the hair extensions.

5

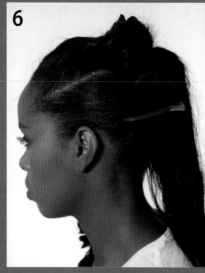

6

7

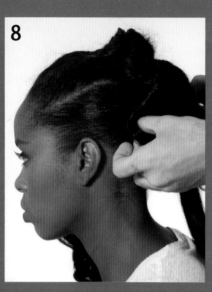

8

9

10

5. Grasp a strand of hair from the lower hair extension and backcomb it to increase volume.

6. Fold the backcombed strand to the left and secure the fold with a hair clip, leaving the ends loose.

7. Gently twist the loose ends of this strand to emphasize the movement to the left.

8. Fold the loose ends of this strand upwards and pin the fold at the top of the head with bobby pins. When you fold the hair, make sure you keep the twist.

9. Gently backcomb the rest of this strand and twist it a bit.

10. Fold this strand of hair again, downwards this time, and affix at the base of the head with bobby pins.

11. Grasp a strand of hair adjacent to the one that you grasped in step 5 and backcomb it to add body.

12. Fold this strand of hair upwards, twisting it slightly, and pin it at the top of the head with a hair clip, leaving the ends loose.

13. Backcomb the loose ends to add body and then gently twist the hair. Fold and affix it with a hair clip. Repeat this process with all of the hair that is loose.

14. Repeat this process with all of the hair in both extensions. Make sure that the folds are similar in size and evenly spaced.

15. Mist the hair with holding spray to keep the folds as tight and smooth as possible.

11

12

13

14

15

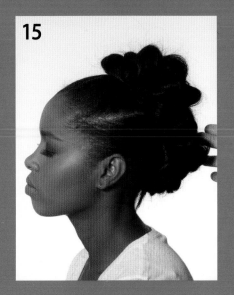

Summertime Swirl

When the living is easy, why not have a hairstyle that's easy too?
This one is filled with gentle twirls and swirls.

1. Wash and blow dry the hair.

2. Make a rounded part at the top of the head to separate the hair at the front of the head from the rest of the hair. Gather this hair in a hair clip and leave the rest of the hair loose.

3. Brush the loose hair upwards and hold it at the back of the head.

4. Wrap a hair elastic around the hair once. Fold the hair over and then secure the fold by wrapping the hair elastic around it again. Leave the long ends of the hair, extending from the hair elastic, down the back of the head.

5

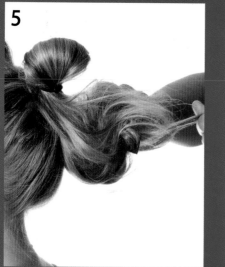

6

7

8

9

10

11

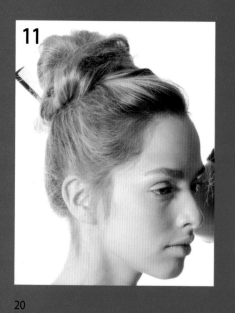

12

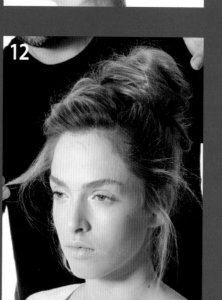

5. Backcomb these ends to add volume.

6. Wrap the ends into a loose, messy bun at the back of the head.

7. Secure the bun with bobby pins.

8. Release the hair at the front of the head and brush it upwards.

9. Backcomb this hair to add volume.

10. Loosely twist the hair around itself.

11. Draw the twisted hair backwards and wrap it around the bun at the back. Secure with bobby pins.

12. Loosen the hair around the face to soften the look and make it even more carefree.

Cinnamon Swirl

Add some spice to your life with this sweet design, filled with twirls, spice and everything nice.

1. Wash and blow dry the hair. Make a half-moon part at the hairline to separate the hair at the front of the head and hold this hair in a hair clip.

2. Start with the hair immediately behind the hair in the hair clip and backcomb it at the roots to add volume.

3. Gently brush back the backcombed hair to create a nice high wave at the top of the head and secure the wave with bobby pins. This will be the base of the design.

4. Grasp a strand of hair behind the left ear and twist it around itself and upwards, drawing it towards the base. Draw the twisted hair over the bobby pins, holding the base in place, and secure with bobby pins.

5. Grasp a strand of hair in front of the left ear and repeat this process, twisting the hair around itself and drawing it towards the back of the head. Pin this twisted strand above the previous one.

6. Grasp a strand of hair from the same side of the head, below the first strand, and repeat the process, twisting the hair around itself and then pinning it at the back of the head, near the base.

7. Now repeat this process on the right side of the head, first twisting and pinning a strand of hair from behind the ear, and then twisting and pinning a strand of hair from above the ear.

8. Grasp a strand of hair from the back of the head, below the base, and affix it at the base.

9. Draw together all the ends of the twisted strands of hair from the left side of the head. Twist these ends together and twirl them into a small bun at the back of the head. Secure the twists with hair clips.

10. Repeat this process with the ends of the twisted strands from the right side of the head.

11. Grasp a strand of loose hair from the back of the head. Twist this hair around itself into a rope, twirl the rope into a bun, and affix at the upper back of the head.

11

12

13

14

12. Twist together the rest of the loose hair at the back of the head into a thick rope.

13. Twist this rope into a bun and affix at the back of the head.

14. Move to the hair at the front of the head. Make a middle part in this hair and then brush the hair on either side of the part backwards. Hold the hair in place with hair clips, mist with holding spray, and then let the hair set for a few moments. Release all the hair clips.

Elegant Allure

This romantic look, lightly twisted and swept away from the neck and face, is perfect for an elegant afternoon affair.

1. Wash and blow dry the hair.

2. Using a curling iron, curl large sections of hair to give it more flexibility and movement.

3. Make a middle part that extends from the hairline to the nape of the neck, dividing the hair into two even sections.

4. Grasp the hair on the left side of the part and twist it tightly around itself, in the direction of the head, to form a rope. Secure the end tightly with a hair elastic.

5. Repeat this process with the hair on the right side of the part, twisting it tightly around itself, in the direction of the head, to form a rope. Secure the end tightly with a hair elastic.

6. Bring the twisted rope on the right side of the head over the top of the head and towards the left ear. Pin the hair just above the left ear and then bring the ends back up and over the head. Pin the ends in place.

7. Repeat this process with the other rope of hair, bringing it from the left side over the top of the head and pinning it above the right ear. Bring the ends back up and over the head, pinning them on the other side.

8. Loosen the hair at the hairline a bit to give the hair at the top of the head a bit of volume.

9. Loosen the hair along both ropes to create a looser, more mischievous look.

Charming Twists

Not sure whether to put your hair up or leave it loose?
This sophisticated twisted ponytail lets you do a bit of both.

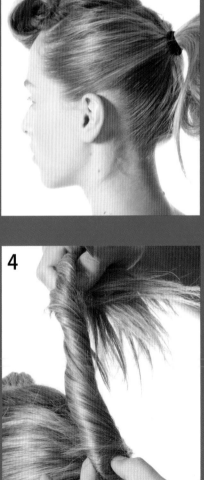

1. Wash and blow dry the hair. Divide the hair into two sections with a half-moon part that extends from above the left eyebrow, around the crown, to the right eyebrow.

2. Secure the hair in front of the part with a hair clip. Secure the hair below the part in a ponytail at the back of the head.

3. Hold the ends of the hair in the ponytail and push the hair towards to head to increase volume.

4. Twist the hair in the ponytail around itself into a thick rope and draw the end of the rope upwards to create a French twist. Hold the twisted hair near the base of the ponytail to tighten the twist.

5

6

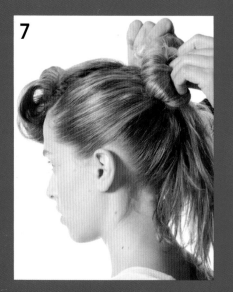

7

8

9

10

5. Twist the hair around the base of the ponytail and secure it with bobby pins.

6. Loosen the hair a bit after each bobby pin is inserted to increase the volume of the twist.

7. Pin only the twisted hair above the ponytail. Leave the ends of the ponytail to hang loose.

8. Gently draw the twisted hair that's above the ponytail to create a half-bun around the top of the ponytail.

9. Release the hair at the top of the head and backcomb it, working on small strands at a time, to add volume.

10. Continue backcombing small strands of hair to achieve maximum volume.

11. Lightly brush the top of the backcombed hair backwards, to smooth the hair without reducing the volume.

12. Twist together the hair that you brushed backwards and tuck it around the left side of the half-bun you shaped in step 8.

13. Secure the twisted hair with bobby pins, leaving the ends loose.

14. Brush out the loose ends of the hair. If you like, curl them with a curling iron.

15. Place a hairband over the top of the head.

11

12

13

14

15

33

Princess Plaits

This soft updo includes an elegant weave at the back combined with lovely loose ends.

1. Wash and blow dry the hair. Divide the hair into two sections with a part that extends from the top of the left ear, over the top of the head, to the top of the right ear. Make a left side part in the front section of hair and gather the hair on the left side of the part in a hair clip.

2. Grasp a small strand of hair at the crown of the head, immediately below the part, and backcomb it to add volume. Repeat this step three more times to add volume at the top of the head.

3. Gently brush back the top of the backcombed hair to smooth the top without reducing the volume. Mist the hair with some holding spray.

4. Grasp three small strands of hair at the hairline, in front of the left ear. Number the strands from left to right: 1, 2 and 3. Bring 1 over 2, and then bring 3 over 1.

5

6

7

8

9

10

5. Re-number the strands so that the rightmost strand is 1. Integrate a bit of hair into 1 and then braid the three strands of hair, as you did in Step 4.

6. Repeat this process until you reach the top of the left ear, integrating a bit of hair into the rightmost strand of the braid every time. After reaching the top of the ear, continue braiding the strands, but without integrating any new strands of hair. Continue until you reach the ends of the hair and then secure with a hair elastic.

7. Curl the loose hair at the hairline with a curling iron to add body.

8. Grasp a small strand of hair at the hairline, between the right ear and the right eyebrow. Draw the strand backwards and secure at the middle back of the head with bobby pins.

9. Leave the hair at the front of the head loose so that it gently frames the face.

10. Loosen the braid a little to make it look more mischievous.

11. Pin the braid at the back of the head with bobby pins.

12. Make a small braid with the hair at the left side of the head and bring it to the back of the head.

13. Draw the small braid on top of the bobby pins that are holding the first braid in place to conceal them. Secure the small braid with bobby pins.

14. Curl the loose hair with a curling iron to add body, and then mist with holding spray.

Bewitching Twist

This gorgeous design is created with a charming crisscross of twists and twirls.

1

2

3

4

1. Wash and blow dry the hair.

2. Make a part to separate the hair at the front hairline from the rest of the hair and secure it in a hair clip.

3. Curl the loose hair, using a large curling iron.

4. Curl the hair at the front as well.

5

6

5. Backcomb the hair at the front to increase volume.

6. Gently brush the backcombed hair backwards so as not to reduce the volume. Hold this hair at the back of the head with a hair clip.

7. Grasp a 1-inch strand of hair at the hairline on the left side of the head. Twist the hair around itself and inwards to make a rope and draw it towards the back of the head.

8. Pin the twisted hair at the middle back of the head.

9. Grasp a similar strand of hair on the right side of the head and twist it to form a rope. Draw it towards the back of the head and over the first twisted rope to form an X.

10. Pin the twisted rope at the back of the head. Repeat this process to twist another strand of hair from the left side of the hair into a rope and draw it towards the back of the head.

7

8

9

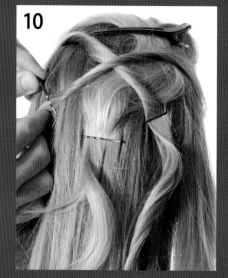

10

11. Repeat the process one more time, this time twisting hair from the right side of the head and pinning it so that it crosses over the other twisted rope.

12. Grasp a strand of hair from the bottom left side of the head. Twist this hair inwards into a rope and pin it at the back of the head.

13. Repeat this process with a twisted rope of hair on the right side of the head.

14. Gather the hair hanging from the twisted ropes at the back of the head. Twist this hair around itself into a rope.

15. Twist the rope into a loop and affix at the back of the head with a bobby pin.

16. Divide the hair hanging loose at the back of the head into left and right sections. Twist the right section around itself towards the right, and the left section around itself towards the left.

17

18

17. Hold the ends of the twisted hair firmly, then bring the left twist over the right twist to form an X.

18. Continue twisting these twisted ropes of hair around each other until you reach the end of the hair, and then secure the twists with a hair elastic.

Twist-a-Licious

Feeling whimsical? Let your playfulness shine through with this playfully twisted design.

1

2

3

4

1. Wash and blow dry the hair.

2. Make a part that extends from just behind the right ear, over the top of the head, to just behind the left ear.

3. Grasp two strands of hair at the middle front of the hairline. Twist the right strand towards the right and the left strand towards the left.

4. Pass the right strand under the left strand.

5

6

7

8

9

10

5. Grasp a small strand of hair on the left side of these strands and twist it into the closest twisted strand. Now pass the other twisted strand under this one.

6. Repeat step 5, twisting a small strand of hair into the twisted strand on the left, and then passing the twisted strand on the right under this strand. Repeat this process, adding a bit of hair to the closest twisted strand every time, to make a long, twisted strand of hair along the left side of the face. Leave a few strands of hair loose for a slightly mischievous look.

7. When the hair you're twisting is no longer adjacent to the scalp, simply twist the two twisted strands around each other until you reach the ends, and then secure with a hair elastic.

8. Backcomb the loose hair at the top of the head to add volume.

9. Grasp a strand of hair from the front right of the head and a strand of hair from the front left of the head. Draw these two strands of hair to the back of the head and join them with a hair elastic.

10. Gather the hair on the upper right side of the head and twist it inwards as you draw it towards the back of the head. Leave a few strands of hair loose at the hairline. Gather the hair on the lower right of the head and twist it around itself. Twist these two twisted ropes of hair together, drawing them to the back of the head.

11.

11. Using a bobby pin, secure the twisted hair at the back of the head, towards the left.

12. Now draw the twist that you made in step 7 (with hair on the front left of the head) towards the back of the head and affix at the same place.

13. Divide the loose hair at the back of the head into two sections. Twist the section on the right around itself and towards the right; twist the section on the left around itself and towards the left.

14. Bring the twisted section of hair on the left under the twisted section on the right, and then bring it over the right twist and then back under it.

15. Continue twisting these two strands of hair until all the hair has been twisted together into a long, thick rope.

16. Wrap the twisted rope around itself into a bun and affix at the back of the head.

17. Loosen the bun by tugging gently on the strands. Mist with holding spray.

Glamour Girl

*And the award for most glamorous updo goes to…you!
Don't wait for an invitation to wear this fashionable design!*

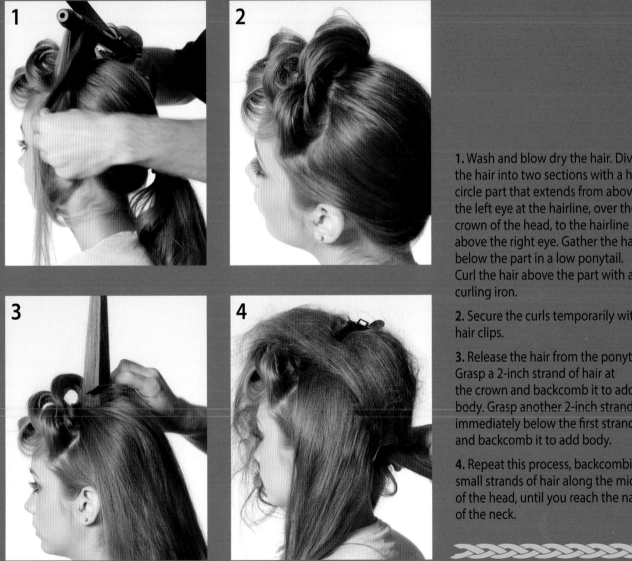

1. Wash and blow dry the hair. Divide the hair into two sections with a half-circle part that extends from above the left eye at the hairline, over the crown of the head, to the hairline above the right eye. Gather the hair below the part in a low ponytail. Curl the hair above the part with a curling iron.

2. Secure the curls temporarily with hair clips.

3. Release the hair from the ponytail. Grasp a 2-inch strand of hair at the crown and backcomb it to add body. Grasp another 2-inch strand immediately below the first strand, and backcomb it to add body.

4. Repeat this process, backcombing small strands of hair along the middle of the head, until you reach the nape of the neck.

5. Now repeat this process along the sides of the head.

6. When all of the hair has been backcombed, brush all of the hair on the right around the back of the head and towards the left side.

7. Secure the hair at the back with a vertical line of bobby pins. Insert the bobby pins so that the open ends face upwards. Start inserting the bobby pins at the nape of the neck and work your way upwards. Insert the last bobby pin at the top, middle of the back of the head. Unlike the other bobby pins, the open end of this pin should face downwards.

8. Brush all the loose hair on the left side of the head towards the back.

9. Twist the hair upwards into a chignon that covers the line of bobby pins.

10. Secure the twisted hair in place with a line of bobby pins.

11. The ends of the hair will now be at the top of the head. Roll them into a thick roll at the top of the head and tuck them under the chignon. Secure the tucked ends with bobby pins to make a large loose bun at the top of the head.

12. Release the hair clips that you used to secure the curled hair in step 1. Grasp a 2-inch strand of hair and backcomb it to add body.

13. Repeat this process with all of the hair at the top of the head, first backcombing it to add body and then brushing it backwards towards the bun at the top of the head.

14. Secure the hair at the top of the head with bobby pins.

15. Arrange the hair to create a styled yet carefree look. Mist with holding spray.

Summertime Romance

Imagine lovely weather, a delicious picnic and this rippling hairstyle.
Perfectly romantic!

1. Wash and blow dry the hair. Make parts to divide the hair into four sections: the top section includes the hair at the front and top of the head; the right section includes the hair behind the right ear; the left section includes the hair behind the left ear; the back section includes the hair at the back of the head. Secure each section of hair with a hair elastic.

2. Release a small strand of hair from the top section of hair and backcomb it to add body.

3. Repeat this process with all of the hair at the top of the head to add volume.

4. Gently brush back the hair at the top of the head to create a smooth, rich appearance. Don't reduce the volume as you brush back the hair towards the ponytail.

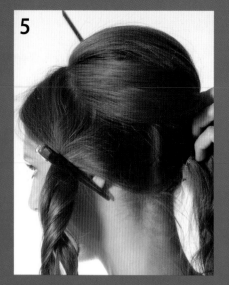

5

6

7

8

9

10

5. Allow the hair to curve into an arc as you draw it towards the back of the head.

6. Affix the hair at the back with bobby pins.

7. Move to the right section of hair. Let the hair at the front of this section hang loose and backcomb the rest of it to add body.

8. Gently brush back the backcombed hair, twisting it slightly, so that it meets the hair you secured in step 6. Secure this hair with bobby pins.

9. Move to the left section of hair. Let the hair at the front of this section hang loose, as you did on the right side.

10. Backcomb the rest of the hair in this section to add volume.

11. Twist the backcombed hair inwards and towards the back of the head, and then secure it at the back with bobby pins.

12. Repeat steps 7 and 8 to backcomb another strand of hair from the right side. Twist the hair towards the back and secure it with bobby pins.

13. Repeat steps 9 and 10 to backcomb, twist and secure another strand of hair from the left side.

14. Twist the ends of the hair around themselves to make small ropes. Allow the twisted ends to coil and then pin them in a decorative pattern at the back of the head.

15. Curl the hair in the ponytail with a curling iron. Mist with holding spray.

Fancy Free

Planning a romantic evening? Create a graceful look to suit the occasion perfectly with this fanciful updo.

1. Wash and blow dry the hair. Divide the hair into two sections with a part that extends over the crown of the head, from the top of the left ear to the top of the right ear. Gather the hair below the part in a low ponytail.

2. Curl the hair at the top of the head with a small curling iron to add body.

3. Bring a small strand of hair from the bottom right of the head, just behind the right ear, to the back of the head. Bring a similarly sized strand of hair from the bottom left of the head, just behind the left ear, to the back of the head. Draw one strand over the other at the back of the head to make an X.

4. Tie the two strands together in a simple knot. Tie them together one more time to make a stable base for the hairstyle.

5

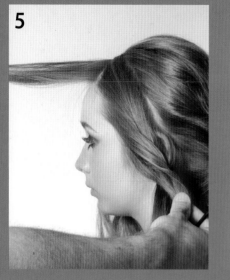

6

7

8

9

10

5. Grasp a small strand of hair at the front left of the head.

6. Twist the hair inwards and around itself to make a rope and draw it loosely to the back of the head. Affix at the back of the head with a bobby pin.

7. Grasp a similar strand of hair at the front right of the head, and twist it into a rope. Secure the hair at the back of the head with a bobby pin.

8. Divide the hair at the back of the head into four equal sections. Secure each section with a hair clip. Grasp the leftmost section of hair and twist it outwards and around itself.

9. Hold the end of the twisted hair with one hand and push the hair up gently to loosen the twist.

10. Wrap the twisted rope of hair above the knot at the back of the head and secure with bobby pins.

11. Repeat this process with the rightmost section of hair, twisting it outwards and around itself, and then bringing it to the back of the head and securing it above the knot at the back with bobby pins. Repeat this process with the remaining two sections of hair.

12. Tuck in all the ends and secure them with bobby pins.

13. Curl the hair at the front of the head with a curling iron to add body.

14. Brush out the curls and then pin the wave backwards with a hair clip. Spray the wave with holding spray. Let the wave stay clipped for about 5 minutes and then remove the hair clip.

15. If you like, finish the look with a pretty floral headband.

11

12

13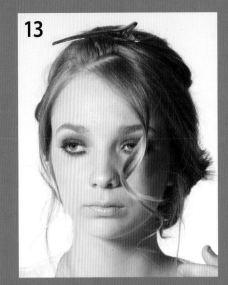

14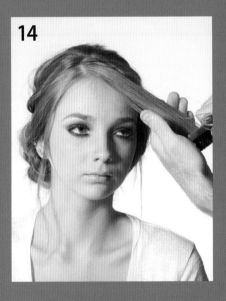

15

Rippling Rapunzel

You don't need a tower to be Rapunzel for a day.
Emphasize really long locks with this rippling design.

1. Wash and blow dry the hair. Make a part that extends from behind the right ear, over the top of the head, to behind the left ear. Curl the hair in front of the part with a curling iron.

2. Gather the hair behind the part and twist it towards the left side of the head.

3. Pin the twisted hair around itself with bobby pins to hold the twist in place.

4. Affix a hair extension just behind the area where the bobby pins are holding the twisted hair in place.

5

6

7

8

9

10

5. Move to the hair at the top of the head and backcomb it at the roots to add volume.

6. Repeat this process with all the hair at the top of the head.

7. Backcomb the entire length of the hair, all the way to the roots, to add volume.

8. Gently brush back the hair to soften the look without reducing the volume.

9. Use bobby pins to secure the backcombed hair just above the twisted hair that you secured in step 3.

10. Divide the hair in the extension into four even strands.

11. Number the strands 1 through 4 and then weave them into a 4-strand braid: bring 1 over 2, 3 over 4, and then 4 over 1. Re-number the strands 1 through 4 and repeat the process: 1 over 2, 3 over 4, and then 4 over 1.

12. Repeat this process until you reach the ends of the hair and then secure the braid with a hair elastic.

13. Gently tug on the strands in the braid to loosen them and increase the width.

14. Loosely fold any loose ends of hair at the back of the head and secure them at the top of the braid with bobby pins.

15. Draw the braided hair over one shoulder and mist with holding spray.

11

12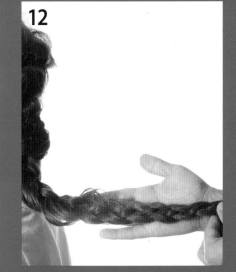

13

14

15

Top Knot

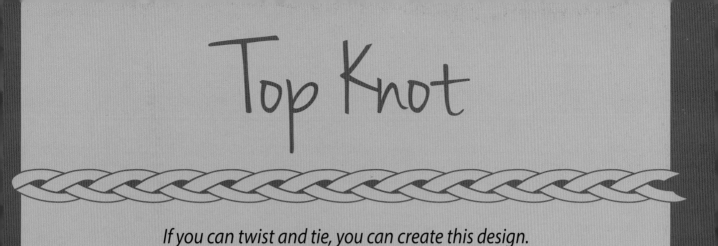

If you can twist and tie, you can create this design.
It's deceptively dramatic!

1. Wash and blow dry the hair.

2. Make a rounded part at the top of the head to separate the hair at the front hairline from the rest of the hair. Gather this hair in a hair clip.

3. Divide the rest of the hair into left and right sections with a middle part that extends from the rounded part you made in step 1 to the nape of the neck.

4. Grasp the hair on the left side of the part and brush it upwards.

5

6

7

8

9

10

11

12

13

5. Twist the hair around itself while holding the ends up to create a thick rope. Hold the end of the hair with one hand.

6. Repeat this process on the other side of the head, twisting the hair upwards and around itself.

7. Tie the two twisted ropes of hair into a knot at the top of the head.

8. Tie the twisted ropes around each other again to make a double knot.

9. Twist the ends of the hair that extend from the knot into little buns and pin them at the back of the head with bobby pins.

10. Release the hair at the front of the head from the hair clip.

11. Brush this hair upwards, twist it and draw the twisted hair backwards.

12. Using bobby pins, affix the twisted hair near one of the buns at the back of the hair.

13. Mist with holding spray.

Fanciful Fishtail

If your hair isn't quite long enough to create the long look you want, integrating extensions is a perfect solution

1. Wash and blow dry the hair. Gather all of the hair in a high ponytail.

2. Attach one hair extension on the top of the head, just in front of the ponytail, using bobby pins.

3. Attach the other hair extension just below the ponytail, using bobby pins.

4. Wrap the natural hair around the base of the ponytail.

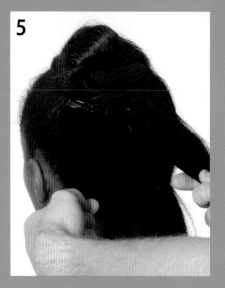

5

6

7

8

9

10

5. Divide the hair in the lower hair extension into right and left strands.

6. Grasp a small strand of hair from the right side of the right strand. Move it over this strand and join it with the hair in the left strand.

7. Grasp a small strand of hair from the left side of the left strand. Move it over this strand, joining it with the hair in the left strand.

8. Repeat step 6, taking a small strand of hair from the right of the right strand and joining it with the left strand.

9. Repeat step 7, taking a small strand of hair from the left side of the left strand and joining it with the right strand.

10. Continue repeating these steps until you reach the ends of the hair to make a fishtail braid. Secure the end of the braid with a hair elastic.

11. Repeat this process with the upper hair extension to make a second fishtail braid.

12. Widen the braids by gently loosening the woven strands of hair.

13. Loosen each braid even more by grasping the end of a braid and gently pushing the hair in the braid upwards.

14. Grasp the top braid and wrap it around the front of the head towards the back, and affix with bobby pins.

15. Grasp the bottom braid, wrap it around the back of the head towards the front, and affix with bobby pins. Once both braids are firmly secured with hair pins, loosen the hair in each braid a bit to give the hairstyle a looser, more relaxed look.

Fishtail Wrap

This updo features fishtail braids wrapped around the head for an elegantly exposed neck.

1. Wash and blow dry the hair. Divide the hair into three sections: the top section includes all the hair from the hairline to the crown, including the hair behind the left ear; the middle section includes the hair immediately behind and above the right ear; the back section includes the hair at the back of the head.

2. Grasp a small section of hair from the top section, at the crown of the head and adjacent to the part with the middle section.

3. Divide this section of hair into two equal strands; a right strand and a left strand.

4. Grasp a small strand of hair from the left side of the left strand. Bring it under the left strand and join it with the right strand. Grasp a small strand of hair from the right side of the right strand. Bring it under the right strand and join it with the left strand.

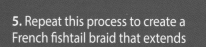

5

6

5. Repeat this process to create a French fishtail braid that extends along the top of the head.

6. Continue braiding in this manner, moving towards the brow as you braid.

7. Allow the braid to turn and follow the hairline towards the left side of the head. Continue braiding behind the left ear and towards the back of the head.

8. Braid the hair all along the hairline, around the back of the head and towards the right ear.

9. When you reach the right ear, stop integrating new strands of hair and make a regular fishtail braid.

10. Continue making a fishtail braid until you reach the ends of the hair.

11. Secure the end of the braid with a hair elastic.

12. Now move to the hair at the front of the head. Divide the hair into three strands and plait them into an ordinary braid.

13. Lift the fishtail braid and bring it over the top of the head, like a hairband.

14. Tug gently on the strands of hair in the fishtail braid to loosen the braid and add volume.

15. Draw the 3-strand braid over the forehead and affix the end to the other side of the head with bobby pins.

7

8

9

10

11

12

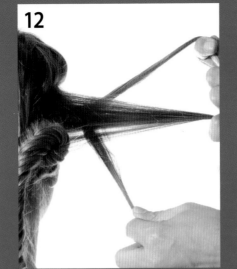

13

14

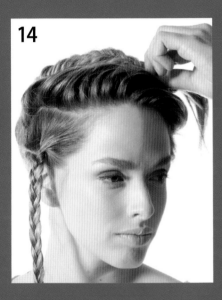

15

Sugar 'n' Spice

With ringlets, braids and twists, this hairstyle has a little bit of everything nice.

1. Wash and blow dry the hair. Make a middle part from the brow to the nape of the neck, and then make a part from the top of the right ear to the middle part. Gather the hair in front of this part in a hair clip.

2. Curl all the loose hair with a small curling iron. Curl the entire length of the hair to make long ringlets.

3. Release the hair from the hair clip on the right side of the head. Divide the hair at the hairline into three even strands. Number the strands 1, 2, and 3, with strand 1 closest to the ear.

4. Make a Dutch braid by bringing 1 under 2, and then 3 under 1.

5. Re-number the strands 1, 2 and 3. Add a bit of hair to 1 and bring it under 2. Add a bit of hair to 3 and bring it under 1.

6. Continue in this manner along this side of the head to integrate all of the hair that wasn't curled in step 2, and then braid the hair into a regular braid. Secure the ends with a hair elastic.

7. Brush out the curls at the back of the head, using a large hairbrush.

8. Brush out the curls at the side of the head as well.

9. Grasp a small strand of hair at the middle front of the head and backcomb it to add body. Repeat with a second small strand of hair at the front of the head, backcombing it to add body.

10. Gently brush back the hair you just backcombed to form a small wave and hold the wave in place with a hair clip. Mist the hair with holding spray and leave clipped for several minutes so that the wave has time to set.

11. Loosen the weave in the Dutch braid a bit by pulling gently at the strands.

12. Wrap the braid around the back of the head and secure it with bobby pins.

13. Tuck the ends under the wrapped part of the braid.

14. Once the wave at the front of the head has set, use a bobby pin to secure the ends, and then carefully remove the hair clip.

15. Mist with holding spray.

11

12

13

14

15

French Fold

Create a modern twist on the classic French twist with this striking design, twisted and folded to perfection.

1. Wash and blow dry the hair.

2. Gather the hair as if you are going to make a high ponytail and then twist it around itself into a tight rope.

3. Secure the twisted rope along the back of the head with bobby pins.

4. Leave the ends of the hair loose.

5. Draw the ends of the hair towards the front right of the head and secure near the hairline with bobby pins.

6

7

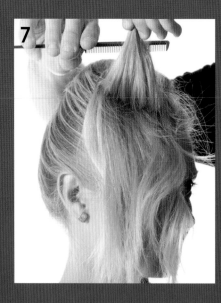

6. Insert bobby pins in a curved line so that all of the hair is secured to the head, while the ends remain loose.

7. Grasp the top layer of hair extending from the line of bobby pins and backcomb it to add volume.

8. Lift all the loose ends and draw them upwards and then backwards.

9. Twist the ends a bit as you draw them back, and then hold in place with a hair clip.

10. Mist the hair with holding spray.

11. Gently brush the sides until they are smooth and in place.

12. Remove the hair clips and replace with bobby pins. Mist with a bit more spray to hold.

8

9

10

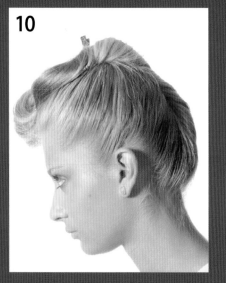

11

12

3

4

5

6

7

8

3. Grasp a strand of hair from the loose hair on the right side of the head and twist it around itself and backwards, towards the backcombed base. Let the twisted hair loop downwards a bit, and then affix it at the base with bobby pins.

4. Repeat this process with a strand of hair from the loose hair on the left side of the head, first twisting the hair around itself and then drawing it backwards towards the base. Affix at the base with bobby pins.

5. Gently backcomb the loose hair at the back of the head to increase volume. Lift all the hair at the back of the head and pin it at the base with bobby pins. Release the hair at the front of the head and backcomb it to add volume.

6. Move to the front left of the head. Make a part to separate the hair at the front hairline from the rest of the hair and leave this hair loose. Grasp the hair immediately behind this hair and divide it into right and left strands. Grasp a small strand of hair from the right side of the right strand and join it with the hair in the left strand. Now grasp a small strand of hair from the left side of the left strand, bring it over the left strand, and join it with the right strand.

7. Add a bit of hair to the right strand and then bring a small section of the right side of the right strand to the left strand. Repeat this process with the left strand. Continue making a French fishtail braid until you reach the ear line and then continue to make a regular fishtail braid with the length of the hair. Secure the end of the braid with a hair elastic.

8. Repeat this process on the other side of the head to make a second fishtail braid.

Fishtail Folly

This playful twist on a traditional fishtail braid results in a lovely textured design.

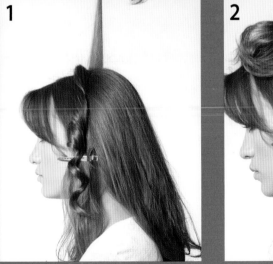

1. Wash and blow dry the hair. Make a part that extends from just behind the right ear, over the top of the head, to just behind the left ear. Hold the hair in front of the part to one side with a hair clip. Grasp a 1-inch strand of hair just behind the part and curl it with a curling iron. Continue curling small strands of hair behind the part.

2. Backcomb the hair at the back of the head to add volume. This area will be the base of the design.

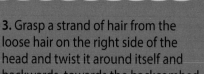

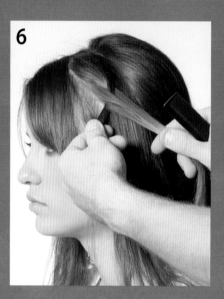

3. Grasp a strand of hair from the loose hair on the right side of the head and twist it around itself and backwards, towards the backcombed base. Let the twisted hair loop downwards a bit, and then affix it at the base with bobby pins.

4. Repeat this process with a strand of hair from the loose hair on the left side of the head, first twisting the hair around itself and then drawing it backwards towards the base. Affix at the base with bobby pins.

5. Gently backcomb the loose hair at the back of the head to increase volume. Lift all the hair at the back of the head and pin it at the base with bobby pins. Release the hair at the front of the head and backcomb it to add volume.

6. Move to the front left of the head. Make a part to separate the hair at the front hairline from the rest of the hair and leave this hair loose. Grasp the hair immediately behind this hair and divide it into right and left strands. Grasp a small strand of hair from the right side of the right strand and join it with the hair in the left strand. Now grasp a small strand of hair from the left side of the left strand, bring it over the left strand, and join it with the right strand.

7. Add a bit of hair to the right strand and then bring a small section of the right side of the right strand to the left strand. Repeat this process with the left strand. Continue making a French fishtail braid until you reach the ear line and then continue to make a regular fishtail braid with the length of the hair. Secure the end of the braid with a hair elastic.

8. Repeat this process on the other side of the head to make a second fishtail braid.

9

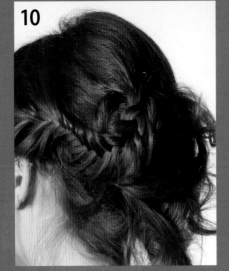

10

11

9. Loosely gather the hair at the back of the head, twisting it around itself and then pinning it at the base of the design.

10. Grasp the braid that extends from the left side of the head and draw it to the back, towards the base. Twist the braid slightly for style and then pin it securely to the base.

11. Repeat this process with the braid on the right side, bringing it to the back of the head and pinning it to the base. Leave some hair hanging loosely at the back to soften the look.

Super Stardom

Remember those gorgeous waves of the 1970s? Recreate the glamour with this luscious hairstyle.

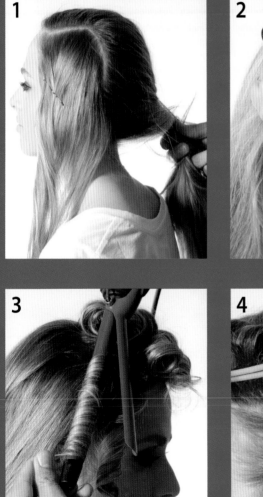

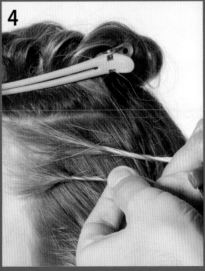

1. Wash and blow dry the hair. Make an L-shaped part that goes from above the left eyebrow, to the crown of the head, and then straight down behind the left ear.

2. Curl the hair at the hairline (on the right side of the part) with a large curling iron to make thick ringlets.

3. Continue curling all of the hair in this manner. Make sure that you curl all of the hair in exactly the same direction.

4. Return to the hair on the left side of the head. Grasp two small strands of hair at the hairline and twist each one of them around itself.

5

6

7

8

9

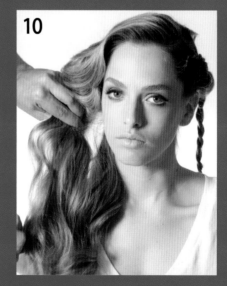

10

5. Draw the top twisted strand over the bottom one to make an X.

6. Hold the two twisted strands of hair together and grasp another small strand of hair at the hairline, just below the first two strands. Twist this strand of hair around itself and then draw it up and over the two twisted strands.

7. Repeat this process, adding a small twisted strand of hair from the hairline every time and integrating it into an ever-growing twisted rope of hair. Continue in this manner until you reach the ends of the hair, and then secure the end with a hair elastic.

8. Mist all the hair with holding spray and let it set for about 10 minutes.

9. Using your fingers, open up the ringlets and loosen the curls.

10. Loosen the curls further by brushing the hair from the roots to the ends of the hair.

11. Backcomb the hair at the roots to add volume.

12. Brush the hair gently and use hair clips to shape and hold the waves in place.

13. Once you've created the waves that you want, mist the hair with holding spray and let it set for several minutes.

14. Draw the rope of hair that you finished in step 7 to the back of the head and secure it to the hair at the back with a small hair elastic.

15. Conceal the connection by brushing the curled hair over it. Mist with holding spray.

11

12

13

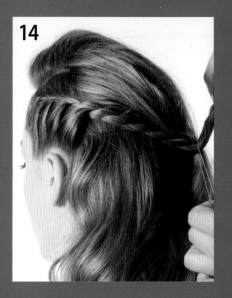

14

15

Creative Crown

Design a funky wrapped crown with two simple braids and some sassy loose strands.

1. Wash and blow dry the hair. Gather it at the back of the head in a high ponytail.

2. Divide the ponytail into two sections. Hold one section with a hair clip and divide the other section into three even strands.

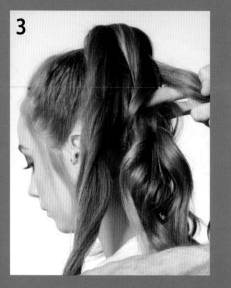

3. Plait these strands into a regular 3-strand braid.

4. Now make a regular braid with the section of hair that you set aside in step 2. Secure the end of each braid with a hair clip.

5. Loosen each of the braids by gently pulling on the plaited hair.

6. Grasp the left braid, draw it to the front of the head, and then wrap it around towards the back. Remove the hair clip and secure the braid in place with bobby pins.

7. Grasp the right braid, draw it to the front of the head, and then wrap it around and towards the back. Tuck this braid under the first braid, remove the hair clip, and secure it with bobby pins.

8. Loosen the plaited hair for a softer, more romantic look. Mist with holding spray.

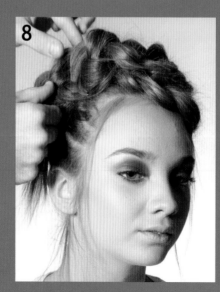

Waves 'n' Braids

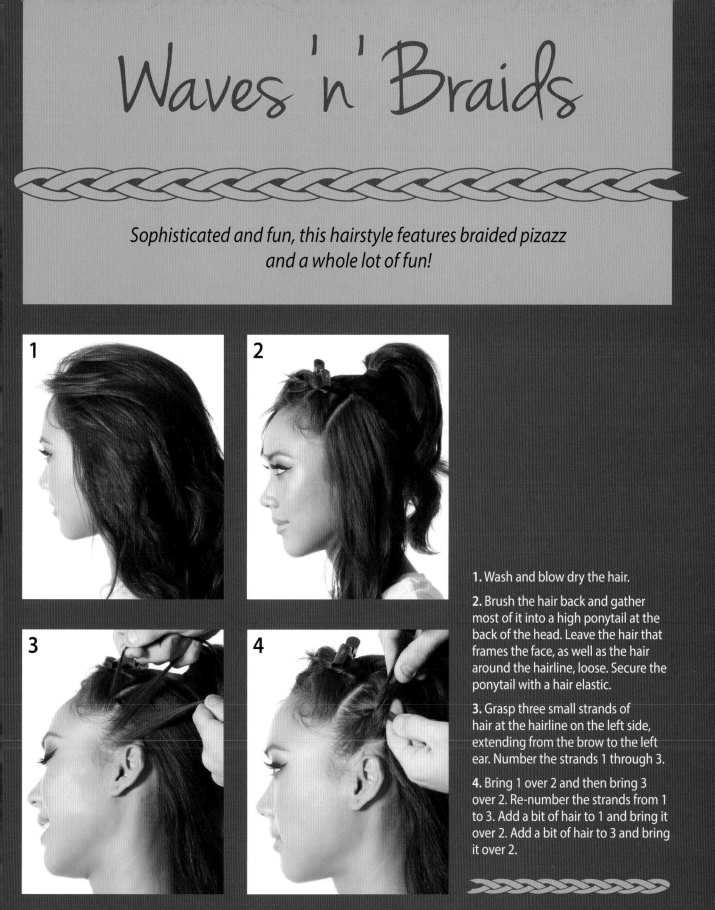

Sophisticated and fun, this hairstyle features braided pizazz and a whole lot of fun!

1. Wash and blow dry the hair.

2. Brush the hair back and gather most of it into a high ponytail at the back of the head. Leave the hair that frames the face, as well as the hair around the hairline, loose. Secure the ponytail with a hair elastic.

3. Grasp three small strands of hair at the hairline on the left side, extending from the brow to the left ear. Number the strands 1 through 3.

4. Bring 1 over 2 and then bring 3 over 2. Re-number the strands from 1 to 3. Add a bit of hair to 1 and bring it over 2. Add a bit of hair to 3 and bring it over 2.

5

6

7

8

9

10

11

12

13

5. Repeat this process to integrate all the loose hair on this side of the head and then braid the hair into a regular 3-strand braid until you reach the ponytail. Affix the braid near the ponytail with bobby pins. Grasp three more strands of hair at the hairline, these ones extending from the top of the left ear to the nape of the neck. Braid these strands in a similar manner, first keeping close to the scalp and then weaving the hair into a regular 3-strand braid, until the braid reaches the ponytail.

6. Affix this braid just below the first braid, at the top of the ponytail.

7. Grasp a strand of hair from the front left of the head and twist it around itself towards the head.

8. Draw the twisted hair backwards and affix it at the top of the ponytail with bobby pins.

9. Backcomb the hair at the top of the head to add volume.

10. Brush the backcombed hair backwards and affix it at the top of the ponytail with bobby pins.

11. Grasp a small strand of hair from the ponytail and wrap it around the hair elastic holding the ponytail to conceal it.

12. Using a large curling iron, curl the hair in the ponytail.

13. After all of the hair in the ponytail has been curled, brush it out to create large thick waves. Use hair clips to secure the waves. Mist with holding spray and then remove the hair clips.

Colossal Curl

The concept is traditional but the implementation is completely contemporary. Classic meets cutting edge.

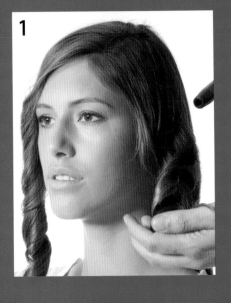

1

2

3

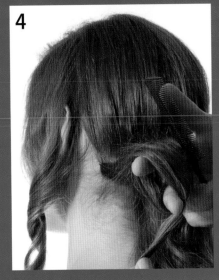

4

1. Wash and blow dry the hair. Make a side part over the right eye and then curl all the hair into ringlets, using a curling iron.

2. Make a part that extends from behind the right ear, over the crown of the head, to behind the left ear. Backcomb the hair immediately behind the part to add volume.

3. Lightly brush back the backcombed hair to create a smooth surface. Secure the hair at the back of the head with a horizontal line of bobby pins, in line with the bottom of the ears.

4. Grasp the hair extending from the bobby pins on the left side of the head and curl it downwards around two fingers to create a thick ringlet.

5

6

7

8

9

10

5. Roll the ringlet upwards towards the line of bobby pins.

6. Place the ringlet over the line of bobby pins to conceal it and then secure it with bobby pins.

7. Repeat this process with the rest of the hair pinned at the back of the head, first wrapping it around your fingers into a ringlet and then securing it with bobby pins over the original row of bobby pins.

8. The ringlets that form the base of this hairstyle should be completely clear and visible.

9. Return to the hair at the front of the head and backcomb the entire length of the hair on the right side of the part.

10. Gently brush the top of the hair to make it smooth but without reducing the volume. Roll the hair around your fingers towards the back of the head.

11. Roll the hair into a thick ringlet and affix the ringlet along the right side of the head with bobby pins. Leave the ends of the hair loose.

12. Grasp the ends of this ringlet and push back the hair with your fingers to add volume.

13. Draw the ends of the ringlet upwards and tuck them into the curl. Secure the ends with bobby pins.

14. Repeat this process with the loose hair on the left side of the head.

15. Mist with holding spray. If you like, complete the design by attaching delicate flowers all around the top of the head.

11

12

13

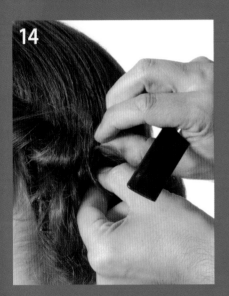

14

15

Extension Extreme

Who says you need long hair for a long hair design?
For best effect, choose extensions that closely match your hair color.

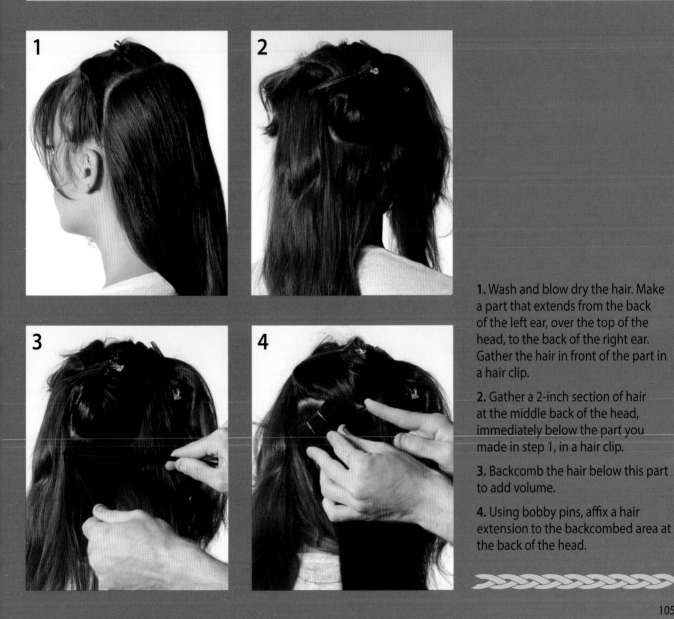

1. Wash and blow dry the hair. Make a part that extends from the back of the left ear, over the top of the head, to the back of the right ear. Gather the hair in front of the part in a hair clip.

2. Gather a 2-inch section of hair at the middle back of the head, immediately below the part you made in step 1, in a hair clip.

3. Backcomb the hair below this part to add volume.

4. Using bobby pins, affix a hair extension to the backcombed area at the back of the head.

5

6

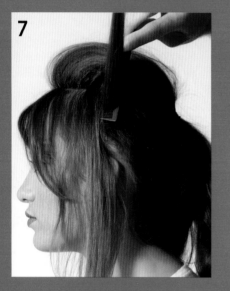

7

8

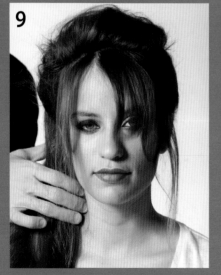

9

10

5. Gather the hair on the left side of the head and twist it backwards. Pin it on top of the bobby pins that are holding the hair extension in place.

6. Release the hair at the front of the head. Starting at the part and moving forwards and towards the left, backcomb the hair in small strands to add volume.

7. Once the hair has been backcombed, gently brush it backwards. Repeat this process with all of the hair on the right side of the head, backcombing small strands of hair every time to add volume.

8. Gently brush back the hair and secure it to the base of the hairstyle with bobby pins.

9. Repeat this process on the left side of the head, drawing the hair backwards and pinning it at the base. Leave some hair hanging loose around the face to soften the look.

10. Grasp a 1-inch strand of hair at the back of the head.

11. Twist the hair around itself into a rope and then let the rope twist naturally into a donut. Pin the twisted hair at the back of the head.

12. Repeat this process two more times to make three twisted ropes at the back of the head. Pin the ropes in place with bobby pins.

13. Divide the remaining loose hair into three strands and braid them into a loose braid that hangs over one shoulder. Mist the braid with holding spray.

11

12

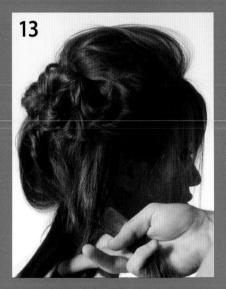

13

Cockle Shells

Evoke the intricate design of a seashell with this twisted and tucked braid.

1. Wash and blow dry the hair. Divide the hair into three sections: the front section includes the hair at the front of the head to the crown; the middle section extends over the top of the head, including the hair from above the left ear to above the right ear; the back section includes the hair at the back of the head.

2. Start with the middle section of hair that extends over the top of the head. (Hold the front and back sections of hair with hair clips for now.) Brush all the hair in this section to the left side of the head. Divide the hair immediately above the left ear into two strands and start weaving the hair into a French fishtail braid.

3. To make this braid, grasp a small strand of hair from the right side of the right strand. Move it over the top of this strand and join it with the hair in the left strand. Grasp a strand of hair to the left of the left strand. Draw it over the left strand and integrate it into the right strand.

4. Continue weaving the hair in this manner to make a braid that extends over the top of the head. Leave the hair at the back and front of the head loose.

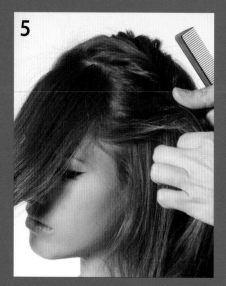

5.

6.

7.

8.

9.

10.

5. As you proceed with the French fishtail braid, the braid will get thicker.

6. Continue integrating hair until you reach the left ear, and then make a regular fishtail braid, joining strands of hair from the left strand into the right strand, and vice versa. Secure the end of the braid with a hair elastic.

7. Now move to the hair at the back of the head. Backcomb the hair at the roots, starting at the top of the section, to add volume.

8. Gently brush the hair upwards so as not to reduce the volume, and then twist the hair upwards into a French twist. Secure the upwards twist at the back of the head with bobby pins.

9. Fold over the ends of the hair at the back of the head and secure them with bobby pins in a loose, relaxed manner.

10. Gently tug on the strands of hair in the braid to loosen and widen the braid.

11. Hold the ends of the braid with one hand and push the braid up, giving the braid a funky, messy look.

12. Fold the braid upwards and affix it at the back of the head with bobby pins.

13. Move to the front section of hair and backcomb it at the roots to add volume.

14. Mist with holding spray to hold the volume.

15. Draw the hair backwards, twisting it around itself to form a rope. Hold the end of the twisted hair and push the twisted hair upwards to increase the volume. Pin the twisted hair at the back of the head and tuck in the ends.

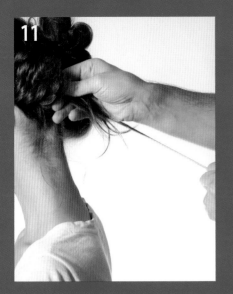

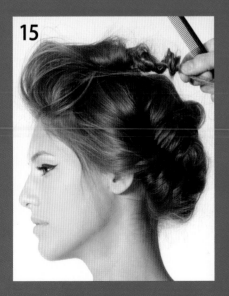

Wild Wreath

Your hair becomes a canvas for creativity in this design.
Decorate with twisted braids and floral accessories.

1. Wash and blow dry the hair.

2. Gather the hair at the crown of the head in a loose ponytail and leave the rest of the hair loose. Make sure you leave the hair at the front of the head loose too.

3. Make a middle part down the back of the hair, from the hair in the loose ponytail to the nape of the neck.

4. Divide the hair along the right side of the part into three vertical strands. Number the strands 1 through 3, with 1 at the top.

5

6

7

8

9

10

5. Bring 1 over 2 so that 1 is now in the middle.

6. Bring 3 over 1 so that 3 is now in the middle.

7. Re-number the strands 1 to 3 and repeat the process, adding a bit of hair to strand 1 before weaving it in.

8. Re-number the strands and continue repeating the process, adding hair to the bottom strand only before weaving it into the braid.

9. Continue braiding the hair all around the head. When you have wrapped the entire head in a braid, make a regular 3-strand braid with the ends and then secure it with a hair elastic.

10. Release the hair in the ponytail at the crown of the head and backcomb it at the roots, working on small strands one at a time, to add volume.

11. Brush the hair upwards and mist with holding spray.

12. Twist the hair around itself while holding it upwards to form a thick twisted rope.

13. Wrap the twisted rope of hair into a bun at the top of the head and affix with bobby pins.

14. Gently loosen the hair in the braid for a looser, more mischievous look.

15. Wrap the long end of the braid around the bun at the top of the head and secure with bobby pins. Mist with holding spray and add a hair accessory, if you like.

11

12

13

14

15

Topsy Turvy

You've spent a lot of time growing your long locks. These carefree braids are a great way of showing them off.

1. Wash and blow dry the hair. Gather the hair at the front of the head in a hair clip. Divide the rest of the hair into four sections; one at the middle front, two on the left side, and one on the right side. Wrap each section into a twist and pin temporarily.

2. Release the hair in the middle front section. Divide the hair at the front of this section into right and left strands. Grasp a small strand of hair from the right side of the right strand. Move it over the top of this strand and join it with the hair in the left strand.

3. Grasp a small strand of hair from the left side of the left strand and move it over this strand, joining it with the hair in the right strand.

4. Integrate a new section of hair into the right strand and then grasp a small strand of hair from the right side of this strand and move it over the strand, joining it with the hair in the left strand.

5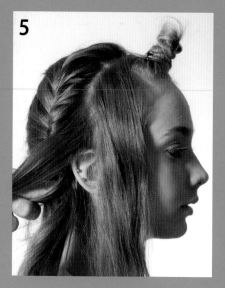

6

7

8

9

10

5. Integrate a new strand of hair into the left strand and then grasp a small strand of hair from the left side of this strand and move it over the strand, joining it with the hair in the right strand. Repeat this process to make a French fishtail braid down the right side of the head. When you reach the top of the ear, start integrating the hair from the strand on the right side of the head.

6. Continue braiding until you reach the end of the hair. Don't worry if some of the hair from the front of the head doesn't get integrated into the braid, as you'll be drawing it backwards later. Secure the end of the braid with a hair elastic.

7. Repeat this process with the bottom left section of hair.

8. Repeat this process one more time with the top left section of hair.

9. Loosen each braid a bit by pulling gently on the braided strands while holding the ends of the braid.

10. Release the hair at the front of the head and twist them inwards while drawing them gently backwards.

11. Pin the twisted hair behind the left ear with a bobby pin.

12. Grasp the loose hair at the front of the head and backcomb it to add body.

13. Gently loosen the braids from the hair framing the face to soften the hairstyle even more.

14. Loosen the braids further by gently tugging on the strands.

15. To finish, mist with holding spray.

Wrapped Around

Create a dramatic, thick bun in this hairstyle by concealing a well-placed hair sponge.

1. Wash and blow dry the hair.

2. Make a part that extends from behind one ear, over the top of the head, to behind the other ear. Hold the hair below the part in a low ponytail. Hold the hair at the middle front of the head with a hair clip. Hold the hair on either side of this hair with hair clips, too.

3. Release the hair from the ponytail. Working on small strands of hair at a time, backcomb the hair at the top of this section to increase volume.

4. Repeat this process all the way down the back of the head.

5

6

7

8

9

10

5. Gently brush back this hair so as not to reduce the volume, and then gather in a low ponytail at the back of the head.

6. Release the hair on the left front of the head.

7. Twist the hair around itself into a tight rope and draw it backwards to the ponytail at the back of the head. Repeat this process on both sides of the head.

8. Wrap a hair sponge around the ponytail at the back of the head and affix it with bobby pins.

9. Curl the hair in the ponytail with a curling iron.

10. Grasp a small strand of hair in the ponytail. Hold the ends of the hair with your fingers and push the rest of the hair towards the head.

11. Draw the ends of the section of hair upwards and pin them to the back of the head, concealing the hair sponge.

12. Repeat this process with all of the hair in the ponytail, first pushing the hair upwards and then pinning it to the head so that it conceals the hair sponge.

13. Repeat this process until all of the hair in the ponytail has been styled and gathered, covering the hair sponge completely.

14. Release the hair at the front of the head and curl it towards one side.

15. Pin this hair to the rest of the hair to style them and then mist with holding spray. Let the hair set for several minutes and then remove the hair clips.

11

12

13

14

15

Licorice Laces

Add a swizzle of life to your hair by incorporating hair extensions for this long design. For a more dramatic look, choose hair extensions that contrast with your hair color.

1. Wash and blow dry the hair. Divide the hair into three sections: the top section includes the hair at the front of the head; the middle section includes the hair from the top of the left ear to the top of the right ear; the back section includes the hair at the back of the head.

2. Brush all the hair in the middle section to the left side of the head and divide it into two equal sections. Twist each section around itself into a rope.

3. Twist the two twisted sections around each other to create a 2-strand rope. Secure the end of the rope with a hair elastic.

4. Move to the top section of hair and make a middle part. Start with the hair on the left and divide it into a top and bottom section. Twist the top section around itself into a rope and secure with a hair elastic.

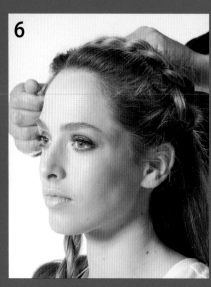

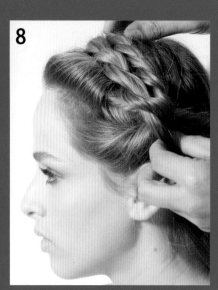

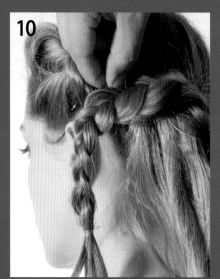

5. Twist the bottom section around itself and draw it backwards. Twist the two twisted sections together into a single thick twist. Secure the twist with a hair elastic.

6. Draw this twisted rope of hair over the top of the head like a hairband and affix it on the other side with bobby pins.

7. Move to the hair at the front right and divide it into two sections. Twist each section around itself and then twist the two sections together.

8. Draw the twisted rope of hair over the top of the head, as you did in step 6, and pin it on the other side of the head.

9. Now move to the back section and divide the hair with a middle part. Secure the hair on either side of the part in a ponytail. Affix a hair extension to each of these ponytails. Grasp a section of hair from one of the ponytails, divide it into three even strands, and make a 3-strand braid.

10. Draw the braid over the area where the hair extension is attached in order to conceal it, and then secure the braid with bobby pins. Repeat this process on the other ponytail.

11. Divide the hair in one of the ponytails into two strands. Twist each strand around itself to make a rope and then twist the two ropes together to make a thick twist.

11

12

13

14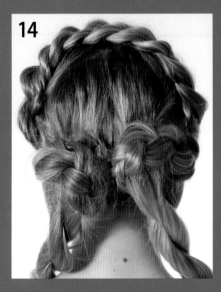

12. Continue twisting the ropes of hair together until you reach the ends of the hair, and then secure the twist with a hair elastic.

13. Repeat this process with the other ponytail, dividing the hair into two sections and then twisting each section around itself to make a twisted rope. Twist the ropes together until you reach the ends of the hair and then secure with a hair elastic.

14. Mist with holding spray.

Braided Tranquility

This braided bun is both elegant and simple. Add delicate white flowers for a thoroughly romantic finish.

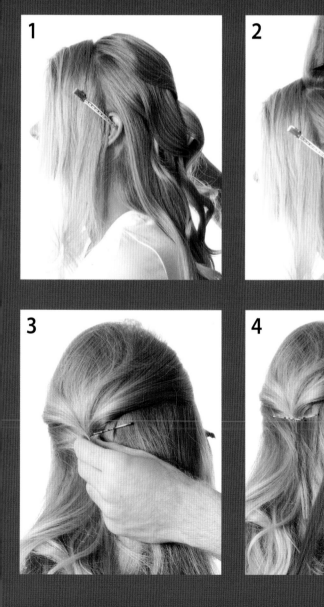

1. Wash and blow dry the hair. Lightly curl the hair with a curling iron to add body. Make a part that extends from the top of the right ear, over the top of the head, to the top of the left ear. Hold the hair in front of the part with hair clips.

2. Backcomb the hair at the top of the head, in front of the part, to add volume.

3. Gently brush back the top of this hair and pin in at the back of the head. This will be the base of the hairstyle.

4. Grasp a 2-inch section of hair at the back right of the head.

5

6

5. Divide this section into three strands and make a regular 3-strand braid.

6. Grasp the hair immediately below this section and twist it inwards and backwards. Secure this twisted hair to the base of the hairstyle.

7. Release the hair at the front of the head and curl it with a curling iron.

8. Grasp a strand of hair from the front left of the head, twist it towards the base of the hairstyle, and secure with bobby pins. Grasp another strand of hair from this side of the head and secure it as well.

9. Draw the hair from the top left of the head in a soft loop around the back of the head and secure it at the base of the hairstyle. Leave a few strands of hair hanging loose to soften the look.

10. Draw the braid that you made in step 5 around the front of the head like a hairband and pin it below the base of the hairstyle, on the left side.

11. Draw the hair from the front right to the back of the head and affix it above the braid.

12. Backcomb the ends of these strands of hair to add volume, and then twist them into a loose bun and affix at the back of the head.

13. Divide the remaining loose hair at the back of the head into two sections. Divide the hair in one section into four strands: number the strands 1 through 4 and braid as follows: Bring 2 over 1 and 4 over 3, and then bring 1 over 4. Re-number the sections from 1 to 4 and bring 2 over 1, 4 over 3, and then 1 over 4. Repeat until you have braided the entire section and secure with a hair elastic. Then make a similar braid in the other section.

7

8

9

10

11

12

13

14

14. Wrap one of the braids around the bun you made in step 13 and affix with bobby pins. Wrap the other braid around this braid and secure with bobby pins. Tuck any loose strands of hair under the bottom of the wrapped braids and affix with bobby pins.

Sassy Swirl

Dare to stand out? This design is sure to make that happen.
If you've got short hair, add extensions for maximum volume.

1. Wash and blow dry the hair. Make a rounded part at the front and secure the hair in front of the part with a hair clip.

2. Brush all the hair on the left side of the head around the back and towards the right side of the head. Hold the hair in place with a vertical line of bobby pins along the middle back of the head.

3. Brush the hair on the right side of the head towards the back and secure it behind the right ear with a line of bobby pins.

4. Twist together all the hair at the back of the head.

5.

6.

5. Fold the twisted hair upwards and pin it at the back of the head, behind the right ear.

6. Affix the hair extension at the back of the head, near the pins holding the twisted hair.

7. Divide the hair extension into two sections. Divide the hair in one section into four strands and prepare to make a 4-strand braid by numbering the strands 1 through 4.

8. Start braiding as follows: Bring 1 under 2 and over 3.

9. Bring 4 over 3 and under 2.

10. Re-number the strands and then bring 1 under 2 and over 3.

11. Bring 4 over 3 and under 2.

12. Repeat this pattern until you reach the end of the hair and secure the end of the braid with a hair elastic. Repeat this process with the other section of hair to make another 4-strand braid. Loosen the strands of the braid a bit to add volume.

13. Coil the first braid loosely around one side of the head and secure with hair pins.

14. Wrap the second braid loosely around the first coiled braid. Tuck the ends of the hair under the coiled braid for a smooth finish.

15. Release the hair at the front of the head from the hair clip and draw it backwards, towards the right ear. Mist with holding spray.

7.

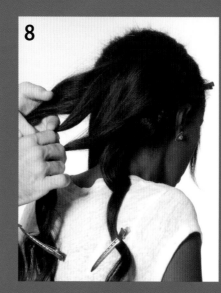

8.

9.

10.

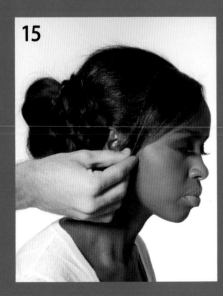

Ripple Effect

Create a rippling wrapped design with this twirled and twisted hairstyle.

1. Wash and blow dry the hair. Make a part that extends from the right ear, over the top of the head, to the left ear. Secure the hair in front of the part with a hair clip.

2. Backcomb the hair at the top of the head to add volume.

3. Gather the rest of the hair in a high ponytail at the back of the head.

4. Gently brush the backcombed hair towards the ponytail. Brush gently to allow for a large wave in the hair, and then secure the hair with bobby pins at the top of the ponytail.

5. Release the hair at the front of the head from the hair clip and divide it into two sections with a left side part. Grasp three small strands of hair along the left side of this part, number them 1 through 3, and braid as follows: bring 1 over 2 and then bring 3 over 1. Re-number the strands 1 through 3 and repeat the process, adding a bit of hair to 1 and 3 just before weaving them to keep the braid close to the scalp.

6. When the end of the braid is aligned with the left end of the left eyebrow, stop integrated strands of hair from the scalp and continue weaving a regular 3-strand braid. Secure the braid with a hair elastic, leaving the loose ends long.

7. Repeat this process with the hair on the right of the part you made in step 5, weaving a smaller braid on the right side of the part. Using a curling iron, curl the hair in the ponytail.

8. Grasp a curled strand of hair from the ponytail. Twist it in the direction of the curl and then backcomb it to loosen it and add volume.

9. Loosely fold the twisted hair and secure it at the back of the head to create a fun, unplanned look.

10. Grasp another curled strand of hair, twist it in the direction of the curl, and backcomb it to add body.

11

12

13

11. Fold the hair upwards and pin it at the back of the head. Repeat this process until all of the hair in the ponytail has been secured at the back of the head.

12. Draw the smaller braid (on the right side of the head) under the gathered hair at the back of the head and secure it with bobby pins.

13. Draw the long braid (on the left side of the head) over the gathered hair at the back of the head and secure it with bobby pins.

Swirl Sensation

There's no braiding at all in this side-swept design—just lots of well-placed swirls that create texture and style.

1

2

1. Wash and blow dry the hair. Divide the hair into two sections with a rectangular part that extends from the left eyebrow straight towards the top of the head, over the crown, and then straight up to the right eyebrow. Gather the hair in front of the part in a hair clip.

2. Draw the rest of the hair to the top right back of the head.

3. Secure the hair with a hair elastic in a high ponytail above the right ear.

4. Grasp the ends of one strand of hair in the ponytail. Hold the ends of the strand of hair with one hand and push up the hair with the other hand to create volume and texture. Repeat this process, one strand at a time, with all the hair in the ponytail.

3

4

5

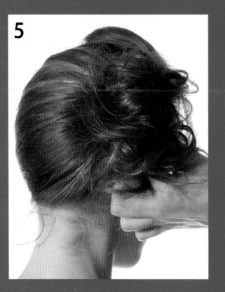

6

7

8

9

10

5. Pin the strands near the base of the ponytail with bobby pins.

6. Arrange the ends of the pushed-back strands so that they swirl and secure with bobby pins.

7. While arranging the hair, strive for a look that isn't too structured.

8. Release the hair at the top of the head and backcomb it at the roots to add volume.

9. Mist the hair with holding spray.

10. Gently brush the hair backwards so that the top is smooth, but without reducing the volume.

11. Roll the hair into a thick twist along the top of the head.

12. Use bobby pins to secure the twist on top of the head, leaving the ends loose.

13. Twist the loose ends around themselves to form a rope.

14. Twist the rope around itself like a cinnamon bun and pin it at the top of the head, just behind the twist you secured in step 12.

15. To soften the final look, gently brush out the ends of the hair.

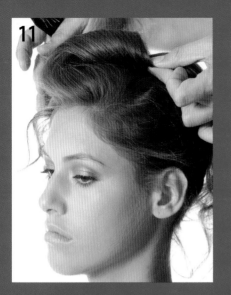

11

12

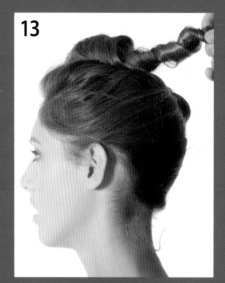

13

14

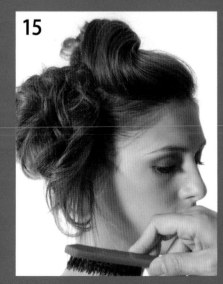

15

Index